AARON RODGERS

Awesome Athletes

Jameson Anderson

Checkerboard
Library

An Imprint of Abdo Publishing
www.abdopublishing.com

www.abdopublishing.com

Published by Abdo Publishing, a division of ABDO, PO Box 398166, Minneapolis, Minnesota 55439. Copyright © 2015 by Abdo Consulting Group, Inc. International copyrights reserved in all countries. No part of this book may be reproduced in any form without written permission from the publisher. Checkerboard Library™ is a trademark and logo of Abdo Publishing.

Printed in the United States of America, North Mankato, Minnesota.
052014
092014

THIS BOOK CONTAINS
RECYCLED MATERIALS

Cover Photo: AP Images
Interior Photos: AP Images pp. 1, 7, 8, 13, 15, 16, 18, 19, 21, 23, 24, 25, 27, 28, 29;
        Corbis pp. 5, 9, 11, 17

Series Coordinator: Tamara L. Britton
Editor: Rochelle Baltzer
Art Direction: Neil Klinepier

Library of Congress Cataloging-in-Publication Data

Anderson, Jameson.
  Aaron Rodgers / Jameson Anderson.
      pages cm. -- (Awesome athletes)
  Includes index.
  ISBN 978-1-62403-335-3
1. Rodgers, Aaron, 1983---Juvenile literature. 2. Football players--United States--Biography--Juvenile literature. 3. Quarterbacks (Football)--United States--Biography--Juvenile literature. I. Title.
  GV939.R6235A64 2015
  796.332092--dc23
  [B]
                          2014002758

TABLE OF CONTENTS

SUPER BOWL MVP

It was February 6, 2011. In Arlington, Texas, the crowd at Cowboys Stadium was on its feet. Cameras were flashing. Fans were cheering for the players who stood on a podium in the middle of the field. Aaron Rodgers had led the Green Bay Packers to a 31–25 victory over the Pittsburgh Steelers in **Super Bowl** XLV.

Rodgers lifted the famous Vince Lombardi Trophy above his head. His dream of winning a Super Bowl had finally come true. And, he was named the game's Most Valuable Player (MVP).

The road to the Super Bowl wasn't easy for Rodgers. There were times when experts wondered if he would ever be a good **National Football League (NFL)** player. He had just proved them wrong.

The Super Bowl victory was the fourth for the Green Bay Packers. Because of all these wins, Packer fans refer to Green Bay, Wisconsin, as Titletown.

FUN FACT THE VINCE LOMBARDI TROPHY IS NAMED AFTER GREEN BAY PACKERS COACH VINCE LOMBARDI. HE COACHED THE TEAM FROM 1959 TO 1967 AND WON FIVE NFL CHAMPIONSHIPS, INCLUDING SUPER BOWLS I AND II.

HIGHLIGHT REEL

Aaron Rodgers was born in Chico, California.

1983

The Green Bay Packers selected Rodgers with the 24th pick in the first round of the NFL Draft.

2005

Rodgers and the Packers beat the Pittsburgh Steelers in Super Bowl XLV; Rodgers was named league MVP.

2011

2003

Rodgers entered the University of California at Berkeley (Cal).

2008

Rodgers became the Packers' starting quarterback.

2013

Rodgers broke his collarbone and was out for seven weeks. He came back and led the Packers to the playoffs.

AARON RODGERS

DOB: December 2, 1983
Ht: 6'2"
Wt: 225
Position: QB
Number: 12

CAREER STATISTICS:

Passing Yards:	24,197
Passing Touchdowns:	188
Rushing Yards:	1,562
Rushing Touchdowns:	18
Quarterback Rating:	104.9

AWARDS:

League MVP: 2011
Pro Bowl: 2009, 2011, 2012
Super Bowl Champion: 2011
Super Bowl MVP: 2011

Aaron Charles Rodgers was born on December 2, 1983, in Chico, California. He was the second son of Edward and Darla Rodgers. Aaron has an older brother named Luke and a younger brother named Jordan.

Aaron had an early interest in football. His father had played college football at California State University in Chico. His career continued in a semi-professional league. There, he had won two national championships.

Aaron was fascinated with football. By the time he was two years old, he would watch entire San Francisco 49ers games on television. Three years later, he could throw a football through a car tire hanging from a tree!

Aaron's brother Jordan is also an NFL quarterback. He played for the Jacksonville Jaguars, the Tampa Bay Buccaneers, and the Miami Dolphins.

Aaron demonstrates his ability to throw a football through a hanging tire before the 2005 NFL Draft.

TALENTED ATHLETE

In elementary school, Aaron also played baseball, basketball, and soccer. His favorite teams were the Los Angeles Dodgers and the San Francisco 49ers.

Aaron's favorite football player was 49ers quarterback Joe Montana. Aaron wanted to play just like Montana. In 1993, the 49ers traded Montana to the Kansas City Chiefs. Aaron was upset that his favorite player was no longer on his favorite team.

In 1994, Aaron's family moved to Oregon. There, Aaron's dad attended the University of Western States. He was studying to become a **chiropractor**.

In Oregon, Aaron mostly played baseball. He played shortstop, center field, and pitcher. With his athletic talent, Aaron could easily compete with older kids. When he was 11 years old, Aaron was named to the 12-year-old league's All-Star Team!

Aaron had the opportunity to present the 2013 NFL MVP award with Joe Montana. Montana won four Super Bowls and was a three-time Super Bowl MVP, a Super Bowl record.

HIGH SCHOOL STAR

In 1997, Aaron's family moved back to Chico. The following year, Aaron entered Pleasant Valley High School. There, he played football, basketball, and baseball. As a senior, Aaron had a 90-mile-an-hour (145-km/h) fastball!

When he was a junior, Aaron became the Vikings' quarterback. That year, he passed for more than 2,000 yards (1,829 m). As a senior, Aaron set a school passing record with 2,303 yards (2,106 m). He also made the All-Section Team as a junior and as a senior.

In addition to athletics, Aaron was active in his community. His parents taught their children that it was important to lead a service-oriented life. Aaron was active in a Christian group for young people called Young Life. He participated in Christian service missions. Aaron also worked for the school athletic department at concession stands.

Pleasant Valley High School students celebrated Aaron Rodgers Day on Friday, February 4, 2011.

OFF TO COLLEGE

In addition to his community service and athletic success, Aaron was a good student. He scored 1310 on the **Scholastic Aptitude Test (SAT)**. Aaron's parents and coaches helped him with his college applications.

However, Aaron did not receive any **scholarship** offers from Division I schools. The Pleasant Valley football team had not won any state championships. College coaches were used to looking for players in larger cities such as Los Angeles. Some coaches didn't believe a small-school quarterback could compete at the elite college level.

In 2002, Aaron decided to attend Butte College, a community college in Oroville, California. He became the Roadrunners' starting quarterback.

As a freshman, Aaron led the team to a 10–1 record. The Roadrunners won the NorCal Conference championship. And, they were the second-ranked community college team in the nation.

Tedford discusses a play with Aaron. Tedford was a two-time Pac-10 Coach of the Year before moving on to coach in the NFL.

Aaron was also spending time in the weight room becoming bigger and stronger. Finally, coaches from bigger colleges began to notice him. One was Jeff Tedford from the University of California at Berkeley (Cal).

Some junior college players have to play for two years before transferring to a Division I school. But Aaron's grades were good and his **SAT** score was high. So in 2003, he entered Cal as a sophomore.

Aaron's 414 yards (379 m) of total offense was a Big Game record.

By the fifth game of his first season, Aaron was the Golden Bears' starting quarterback. Aaron didn't waste his opportunity. He started his career at Cal by throwing 98 passes in a row without an interception!

The Golden Bears' final game of the season was against rival Stanford University. The two schools had been facing each other in the Big Game for 106 years. On November 22, 2003, Aaron led the Golden Bears to a 28–16 victory to claim the Stanford Axe.

The Bears ended the season 7–6. The team was selected to play the Virginia Tech Hokies in the Insight Bowl. The nationally televised game gave Aaron exposure to **NFL scouts**. Aaron threw for 394 yards (360 m) in a 52–49 win. He was named the game's MVP.

Though the Golden Bears lost to USC his junior year, Aaron set a school record during the game with 23 completed passes in a row.

Aaron's junior year at Cal was even more impressive. He led the Golden Bears to a 10–1 record. The team's only loss was to rival University of Southern California (USC), 23–17.

After the season, the Golden Bears faced Texas Tech in the Holiday Bowl. Almost everyone thought Cal would win easily. But Texas Tech surprised them with a 45–31 win. At this point, Aaron had a decision to make. Should he stay at Cal for his senior year, or enter the NFL **Draft**?

THE NFL

Rodgers decided to bypass his final year at Cal and enter the 2005 **NFL Draft**. He was one of the best quarterbacks in college football. Experts expected Rodgers to be an early selection.

Rodgers runs the 40-yard (37-m) dash at the 2005 NFL Combine.

Though Rodgers dropped to number twenty-four in the draft, he was the second quarterback selected.

The **draft** began on April 23, 2005. Many experts thought Rodgers's childhood favorite, the San Francisco 49ers, would take him with the draft's first pick. Instead, the 49ers took Alex Smith from the University of Utah.

Rodgers watched as 22 more players were drafted ahead of him. Finally, the Green Bay Packers made Rodgers the twenty-fourth pick.

Rodgers was happy for the opportunity to play in the **NFL**. But the Packers had the same starting quarterback since 1992. Brett Favre was a legend. He was a **Super Bowl**-winning quarterback who rarely got hurt. Rodgers's hopes of being a starter in the NFL had to be put on hold. Favre wasn't going anywhere. Or was he?

Favre had hinted in 2006 and 2007 that he would retire. But each year, he returned to play. Finally in March 2008, Favre retired. Then he changed his mind and wanted to rejoin the team. But the Packers were ready to move on. Favre was traded to the New York Jets.

On September 8, 2008, Rodgers played his first game as Green Bay's starting quarterback. The Packers won 24–19 over the rival Minnesota Vikings. That season, Rodgers completed 341 of 538 passes for 4,003 yards (3,660 m) and 28 touchdowns.

Despite Rodgers's success, the Packers did not make the **playoffs**. They went 6–10 for the season. But the Packers rewarded Rodgers's performance with a six-year, $65 million contract extension.

In 2009, Rodgers was 350 of 541 for 4,434 yards (4,054 m) and 30 touchdowns. The team ended the season 11–5 and made it to the playoffs. There, they met the Arizona Cardinals in the divisional round.

The Cards ran back this fumble by Rodgers for the game-winning touchdown.

Rodgers was 28 of 42 for 423 yards (387 m) and four touchdowns. He also scored one rushing touchdown. Rodgers's total passing yards was an **NFL postseason** team record. But the Cards edged the Pack for a 51–45 win. The game was the highest-scoring **playoff** game in NFL history. But the loss meant the Packers missed the playoffs that year.

SUPER SEASON

The Packers started the 2010 season strong. The team was 6–3 going into the **bye**. But Rodgers had suffered a **concussion** in a loss against the Washington Redskins. He endured a second in another loss to the Detroit Lions. Rodgers was out for two games.

Even with Rodgers's injuries, the Packers finished 10–6 and made the **playoffs**. A 21–16 win over the Philadelphia Eagles and a 48–21 victory over the Atlanta Falcons put the Pack in the NFC Championship game. There, they faced the Chicago Bears.

The Pack had beaten the Bears 10–3 in Week 17. A win here would send the team to the **Super Bowl**. Rodgers was back in the starting position and completed 17 of 30 passes for 244 yards (223 m). He threw no touchdown passes and tossed two interceptions. However, he scored one of the Pack's three rushing touchdowns for a 21–14 win.

Rodgers had seven rushes for 49 yards (45 m) against the Bears, and scored a rare rushing touchdown.

The Packers were set to play the Pittsburgh Steelers in **Super Bowl** XLV. Rodgers was 24 of 39 for 304 yards (278 m) and three touchdowns in the 31–25 win. He was named MVP and finally made his own place in **NFL** history.

Rodgers has had successful seasons since leading the Packers to the Super Bowl in 2010. In 2011, the Packers

Rodgers celebrated his Super Bowl win with his family including *(L to R)* brother Jordan, father Ed, mother Darla, and grandparents Chuck and Barbara Pittman.

started the season 13–0. They lost to the New York Giants in the divisional round. But Rodgers completed 343 of 502 passes for 4,643 yards (4,246 m) and 45 touchdowns that year. His performance earned the league MVP award.

INJURY CHALLENGE

In 2012, the Packers again made it to the **playoffs**. Yet they lost in the divisional round, this time to the 49ers, 45–31. On April 26, 2013, the Packers and Rodgers agreed to a 5-year, $110 million contract extension. He became the highest-paid player in **NFL** history.

But the season didn't go as planned. On November 4, 2013, Rodgers was sacked by Chicago Bears **linebacker** Shea McClellin. Rodgers broke his collarbone, which impaired his arm motion. The Packers lost the game 27–20. Rodgers was out of action for seven weeks.

On December 29, the team met the Bears once again. Though he had been out with a major injury, Rodgers led the Packers to a 33–28 win on a 25-of-39, 318-yard (291-m) passing performance. The Packers made it to the playoffs. But again they lost to the San Francisco 49ers, 23–20.

McClellin's tackle drove Rodgers's left shoulder into the ground and broke his collarbone.

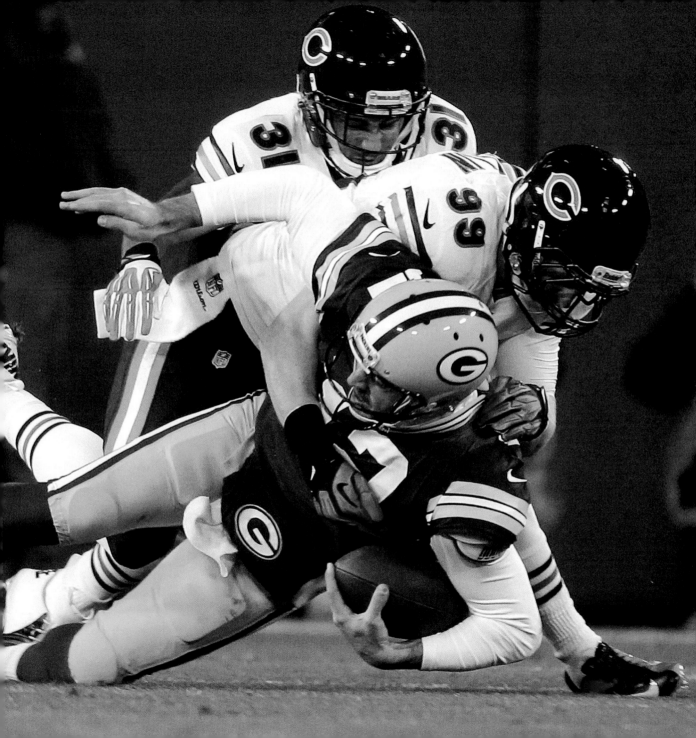

Rodgers putts in the American Century golf tournament. To date, the tournament has raised more than $4 million for charities.

During the off-season, Rodgers continues the life of service he began as a boy. He still works with Young Life, hosting a charity golf event. In addition, Rodgers plays in the annual Andy North and Friends Golf Getaway. This event raises money for the Paul P. Carbone Comprehensive Cancer Center.

In 2010, Rodgers participated in the Salvation Army's Twelve Days of Christmas. During this event, kids were able to go holiday shopping, eat pizza, and hang out with their favorite Green Bay Packers.

Midwest Athletes Against Childhood Cancer supports research in curing childhood cancer and blood disorders. This organization was featured in Season One on it'sAaron. Rodgers began it'sAaron with David Gruber. It brings attention to individuals and organizations that are working to improve Wisconsin communities.

Each season Rodgers leads the Packers to the **playoffs**, they have another chance of making the **Super Bowl**. Can Rodgers lead the team back to the big game? Time will tell!

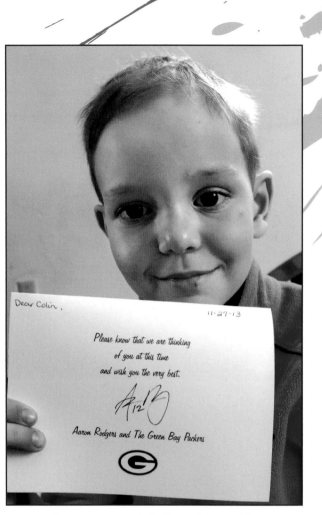

Cancer patient Colin Cahill holds a card he received from Rodgers.

GLOSSARY

bye - a week during which a team does not play a game.

chiropractor - a doctor who treats people who are sick or in pain by adjusting body structures.

concussion - a brain injury caused by a blow to the head.

draft - an event during which sports teams choose new players. Choosing new players is known as drafting them.

linebacker - a defensive player who can defend both running and passing plays.

National Football League (NFL) - the highest level of professional football. It is made up of the American Football Conference (AFC) and the National Football Conference (NFC).

playoffs - a series of games that determine which team will win a championship.

postseason - the time immediately following the regular season when teams play each other to determine which teams are in the playoffs.

scholarship - money or aid given to help a student continue his or her studies.

Scholastic Aptitude Test (SAT) - a test that is intended to evaluate a student's readiness for college.

scout - a person who evaluates the talent of amateur athletes to determine if they would have success in the pros.

Super Bowl - the annual National Football League (NFL) championship game. It is played by the winners of the American and National Conferences.

To learn more about Awesome Athletes, visit **booklinks.abdopublishing.com**. These links are routinely monitored and updated to provide the most current information available.

INDEX